Lamentations
of the Heart
Mingled with Peace and Joy

Marti Wells-Smith

For information, contact
MSI Press
1760-F Airline Highway, #203
Hollister, CA 95023

Cover designed by Carl Leaver
Cover Photograph by Ruslan Huzau/ShutterStock
All Interior Art by Likius/Shutterstock

Copyeditor: Mary Ann Raemisch

Permission to use "Old Woman of Carey Street" given by *Gifts of Words*.
.
Library of Congress Number: 2021900001

ISBN: 978-1-950328-75-8

In loving Memory of Grant Wells

Child of God
Beloved son
Loyal family member
Friend to many

Marti Wells-Smith

Contents

Marti Wells-Smith

With a Grateful Heart
Author Acknowledgements

I deeply appreciate and thank the following individuals and groups for their many acts of kindness during the initial time of my loss and for providing additional support and services to assist me in the making of this book:

Above all, my Heavenly Father, Who has carried me through the valley of the shadow of death and has profoundly gifted me with the signs and wonders that I share in *Lamentations of the Heart.*

My husband Scott, who shares my sorrow as we recall many happy memories and has been a source of strength and love without fail. His assistance with technical matters has been a Godsend.

Sisters in Christ, Carolynn Strickland-Hickman and Carolyn England, for proofreading, constructive commentary, and much needed emotional support and intercessory prayer.

Dear friends, gathered from many places, who have lifted me up and sustained me again and again.

Christian brethren from my Facebook and on-line support groups, who provide prayerful compassion and grace when needed.

My GriefShare group, who helped me to process my loss and to embrace all that is good in my daily life.

Extended family, who responded with empathy and concern, showing me the bond that connects us is powerful and transcends all differences.

Shepherd's Chapel, my church, which has taught me the importance of studying the Word more deeply. Although the more contemporary New Revised Standard Version (NRSV) has been used for the purposes of this book, the King James Version (KJV) and Strong's Concordance provide correct translations from the original Bible manuscripts in conjunction with other important works by a host of well-known scholars that are available from the Shepherd's Chapel library.

To Those Who Have Opened This Book

In these pages, you will read of the loss of my only child. I share the details not to inflict needless pain—but rather, to share the incredible signs I received assuring me that he is safe in heaven. The circumstances were shocking, but had miraculous consolations. I was so overwhelmed with them all that I felt compelled to express my emotions in both poetic and prose form, while honestly conveying the facts as they unfolded.

As believers, we know that the innocent young always ascend to their heavenly homes upon passing. But perhaps you have also lost an adult child, or other loved ones—and are concerned about their eternal well-being. If so, then I have written this book for you. The Lord has led me to this place—where I discovered, in the midst of my loss, that our heavenly Father is more loving and compassionate toward all of His children than I could possibly have imagined.

Lamentations of the Heart delves into many aspects of my life and the lives of some of the people I've encountered as I prayerfully tried to understand how everything fits together within the tapestry of my existence and purpose. The book then returns to the passing of my son and all that it brought to the forefront of my life.

I know that countless numbers of us have experienced tremendous loss and have struggled to move forward in faith. I'm relying on God and searching His scriptures as I write my thoughts and explore the deepest parts of my being. I feel led to share my words with other Christians who are searching for hope in what seems like a hopeless situation concerning their departed loved ones.

As my heart heals, my writing has reflected the entire gamut of emotion, going back and forth and up and down. There is no certain way to deal with grief—it takes on a life of its own in the process of recovering. Needless to say, we are never the same. How could we be? But faith moves me forward and sustains my heart, including moments of peace and joy.

As I continue to reach out for the lasting comfort that only our Lord can provide, I pray that you, too, will find solace within these pages...

Lamentations 1:12 Look and see if there is any sorrow like my sorrow, which was brought upon me.
Lamentations 3:22 The steadfast love of the Lord never ceases, his mercies never come to an end.

MOTHER OF MEMORIES

A JOYFUL CRY

The day reminds me of another,
with streaked blue sky and splatters of sun.
A lone pink tulip leans my way
with a centered, black design;
open, like my heart.
You were there that day,
smiling in the moment.
I still see you as that sweet, careless boy;
my son, young and hopeful—
the hopelessness to come, several years out.
Our yard, puddled with early morning rain
was your splashing ground, amid childish shouts.
How I wish we could live it again…
Yet hope in Christ remains.
I will see you once more
and greet you with a joyful cry.
The years I have waited
will disappear, like old rain on a sunny day.
And again, you will be mine.

John 14:2 "In My Father's house there are many dwelling places. If it were not so, would 1 have told you that I go to prepare a place for you?"

SUPPERTIME ON EARTH

I fix your favorite today, here in our kitchen, worn old with use, as the late afternoon turns violet and pink. Beyond the sink window are hot shimmering hues with finger shaped streaks that point to my gaze. The table a maze of cookware and glass that spreads itself wide to finish my task.

I mix salt and flour, spice and tears. This gathering room, gracious and dear, once gave us its very best years. Filled with pasta and bread, the toasting of wine, sauces to simmer and offer a taste, blackberry cobblers to sweeten and bake. I see a thousand meals in making this one today. Egg souffles in sunlight or a white-gray day of gloom. We lived in those moments, as family, here in this room.

The back door opened to your voice as we welcomed you home. You always returned when the world became bland or anything but good, when the smallest parts of life could not be understood. And there I was, as I long to be now—arms outstretched in greeting. You watched as I stirred upon the stove, my humble way to please. It was the only kind of hunger that I could hope to ease. Oh, the making of it all, the savor.

I once made you, my son, on a dark Oklahoma night. Unknowingly, without thought or plan, you were added to my life. God looked down as the years moved on like faces in a dream. It would never be enough for me—or so it somehow seemed—for in a darkened purple dawn, you were taken from this place, this home of simmering food provided by His grace. Questions somehow mix well within a mother's faith. I look up, lovingly, into a sky of violet hues as I make your favorite dish today, here on earth, in our kitchen worn old with use.

Psalm 107:9 For He satisfies the thirsty, and the hungry He fills with good things.

THE INVENTOR OF TEARS

As my tears fall, quick and soft,
I lift them up to You.
You, my LORD, the Omniscient One,
will keep them for me.
It is written,
it is promised.
They will not go to waste,
held in a bottle
in a heavenly place—
where You consider the reasons
and acknowledge the meaning.
You, the Inventor of tears,
help me release all that I hold inside.
You find it precious in Your sight,
the evidence of great emotion
that diminishes pain,
that heals from within.
It is a priceless gift, Father
and I use it again and again.

Revelation 21:4 He will wipe every tear from their eyes.
Death will be no more; mourning and crying and pain will be
no more, for the first things have passed away.

MINE ALONE

My beautiful, exquisite pain, mine alone, glows and shimmers, pelting in a private rain—the depth of it, the width, its reflection in the mirror, the shadow, the gleaming each time that it draws near. There is nothing new under the sun. This my soul knows well. Yet, my loss is new to me, rich and fresh, darkest blue and golden, with a multitude of thoughts that I can never share. It captures me as I arise, as I close my eyes to sleep, as I go through my day with something more compelling than mere grief.

For blessings and peace meld with it, such goodness to recall. Then the darkened blue sets in, only to begin its pelting—as hail upon sheets of tin. I contemplate your end and I, too, am stopped, held, moved backward in longing. Peering beyond the room, the day, unable to see anything but my captivating loss that lingers into the night, that has invited itself to stay.

I spin inwardly, wordlessly. Then return to my listless couch. I must accept and trust, step forward in faith, regardless of why or how. I was blinded to what approached, deaf to its loud warning. Assuming prayers would blend my plans into the very will of God. Yet, there is no bitterness. Does the clay command the potter when it cannot see its end? Should a child of the King cry foul when she cannot comprehend? No, I cry mercy. I cry hope. As my new companion wraps me in its arms and holds me close. My beautiful, exquisite pain, mine alone.

Psalm 147:3 He heals the brokenhearted and binds up their wounds.

ALMOST

Almost everything reminds me of you,
a child across the street,
for you were once my child—
a smiling stranger too,
although you never really knew one.
You smiled back, as a friend;
rendering action and adventure
with a few wrong turns here and there.
Still, a kindly hero riding through the night
to rescue all but yourself
in the course of your short life.
Music, sounding from the radio—
you sang to it, moved with it,
slept with it, on low.
The pulsing of the sun, the peppering of stars,
you lived beneath them,
as no other.
Now you are up there, among them,
returned to God; while here I remain,
your loving mother
who has grown to accept it.
Almost...

Ephesians 2: 4-6 But God, who is rich in mercy, out of the great love with which He loved us even when we were dead through our trespasses, made us alive together with Christ— by grace you have been saved—and raised us up with Him and seated us with Him in the heavenly places in Christ Jesus.

THE GREATER OF THE TWO

Grant Daniel Wells July 12, 1993 – June 21, 2019

It is written in *Ecclesiastes* 7:1 that the day of our death is greater than the day of birth. I contemplate this, as I continue to heal and come to terms with the unexpected loss of my only child, Grant. He was almost 26 when he passed away. He had been ill and had come home for a visit before seeking further medical help. None of us, including him, realized how serious his illness was. He had been bitten by a spider near his heart while on a pipeline job in Pennsylvania. He went to a hospital, was treated, and spent a couple of days resting in his motel room.

He finished work, told us he felt better, and drove back to Kansas. He was an uninsured contractor, but he had full medical coverage through Indian benefits in Oklahoma just a couple of hours away. The plan for more treatment as needed relied on those benefits.

In retrospect, Grant looked bloated when he walked through the door; I assumed he had gained weight eating junk food on the road. His appetite, however, was off, and he was experiencing some swelling and low energy. I've gone over and over the details since I found him in his bed.

My husband had been bitten by a brown recluse years ago, which occasioned a couple of trips to the ER, months of recovery, and the same symptoms that Grant was having. All this gave me a false sense of security, that he would recover. Yet, my son was dying that week as he played golf, went to a birthday party, grilled for us on Father's Day, and checked in with friends around town. One of them, who was studying to be a nurse, told me later that he didn't look right, and she had told him to see another doctor immediately. Grant, though, was homesick and wanted to stay around long enough to see everyone.

"I'm going in a day or two. I'll be fine." I was reassured when he kept saying, "Mom, it will be OK. "

He had gassed up his truck the night before it happened, He planned to head out the next morning for the Oklahoma prairie to stay at his dad's place and get another checkup. Only he didn't make it. I've wondered if there was anything I could have said or done that would have changed the out-come. It's written in *Psalm* 139 that our days are numbered. Was it really Grant's time? Would it have happened in his 25th year one way or another?

We have a studio apartment out back, where he had briefly lived while attending the local community college. It had become his place whenever he was home. We spent our last hour together there, playing a board game as we visited. Grant was a big, handsome man with a beautiful smile, but he hid a lot of pain behind that smile.

"I'm getting ready to turn 26, then I'll be 30, and then..."

His eyes looked sad that night, and I heard no enthusiasm in his voice. He sometimes let his guard down, and I would see glimpses of his true feelings. He had lost in the pursuit of love, and more than once. He watched many of his friends marry and start families. He became Uncle Grant, still flash-ing his smile to one and all—while privately he struggled with frustration and hurt. I knew some of it and kept him in prayer. *Lord, please bless him with a loving woman, who will help him grow in his faith. Please help him to make good decisions and secure his future.*

Grant was a young Christian who hadn't studied the Word at a deeper level yet and grappled at times with the unfairness of life and how God figured in with it all. He re-sented the fact that he had old sports injuries that kept him in varying degrees of pain. He was 6'2" and large boned, close to 290 pounds, but quite handsome, with dark blonde hair, big blue eyes and a dazzling smile complete with dimples—

which had won him Best Smile his senior year. Yet he was humble by nature, and well aware of what he perceived to be flaws, usually wearing a hat or cap to hide the fact that his hair was thinning, yet another issue that bothered him.

He confided in me how upset he was when his dad lost a well-paying ranch position and how difficult it was to deal with the aftermath. Grant wanted to own cattle and share an operation, but it wasn't possible without a large amount of start-up money. After trying a couple of jobs that didn't work out, he hoped his contractor earnings would help raise the cash. That was his dream.

In the meantime, he continued to question why certain things were allowed to happen. I tried to explain that we're all only passing through this life.

"Son, there will be trials for each of us along the way. We're not in heaven yet."

He held my hand and accepted Christ as his Savior when he was 11 years old. He was baptized at 13. By the end of his 15th year, he chose to return to Oklahoma to live with his dad and finish high school there. He missed the country life and wasn't happy with some of the issues at the school in our town. I wept at first but decided to graciously let him go. Although we would see each other regularly and text or call often, I had relinquished my position as the custodial parent and wasn't sure if I could have an impact on how he grew as a Christian from that time on.

Until his 12th year, I had always tucked him into bed, said prayers with him, and sang a medley of *Jesus Loves the Little Children*, *You Are My Sunshine*, and *Jesus Loves You Most of All*, a little song that I had made up for him as a toddler. When puberty began, this ritual was replaced with a reminder to brush his teeth and say his prayers.

"Good night. Love you, Mom."

"Love you too, son. Sweet dreams."

It all seems like a dream to me now. Grant was feverish that final night and told me he had taken some ibuprofen. He also mentioned feeling weak and exhausted. It didn't register with me, as if a veil had been placed over my ability to comprehend. I turned to him as he sat in the recliner and suddenly felt a desire to anoint him for healing although I hadn't offered before, and he seemed a little uncomfortable with the idea. I had always covered him in prayer and scripture and at times, taken communion and anointed by proxy for him, waiting for his faith to reach a point where he would understand the significance of it.

That night, I looked at him and said, "I have enough faith for both of us."

I walked to the main house quickly and returned with my container of olive oil. He closed his eyes as I touched his forehead.

"Be healed in Jesus' name."

It was the last time that I would touch my son while he was alive in the flesh. How I wished I had hugged him that night and told him again how much I love him. But he knew. He always knew. He stumbled to his bed, and I remember thinking it would be good for him to rest before his trip the next day.

"Mom, I just need to lie down and sleep and sleep."

Those are the last words of his that I can recall. I walked to the door and turned back to him as he was covering up.

"Your body is telling you that it needs to rest."

Then, I locked the door behind me. Unknowingly, without another parting comment, it became my good-bye. I watched some TV, finished my nightly routine, read some scripture, and went calmly to sleep, hoping my son was resting, too.

Grant had spent a couple of nights with a contractor friend out in the country. Because he mentioned that he hadn't slept well, I attributed much of his exhaustion to that. I checked on him around 10 the next morning when I unlocked the door to let our two cats out. Grant loved animals, and they were drawn to him. He had been living in motels for over a year while traveling. Pets weren't an option in motels at the time so he enjoyed their company whenever he got the chance.

He had left a muted light on, and the TV was still going. I glanced at him, lying in the bed at the other end of the room. His covers were off and he was on his back, arms to each side. He looked very peaceful. I thought he was finally getting a good sleep, and shut the TV off before I locked him back in. I left to run errands, and it wasn't until later in the afternoon that I became concerned. I texted him a couple of times with no response. It seemed odd, and I told my husband that I was going back out to check on him again.

I knocked on the apartment door, then opened it and peeked in. My first thought was, *He hasn't moved.* I walked to the side of his bed and really looked at him. His eyes were closed. He was pale and didn't look like he was breathing. I called his name. Nothing. I started to feel for his pulse but touched his cheek instead. My beautiful son, my only child, felt very cold.

I ran to the house, screaming, "Scott! Scott! I think Grant's dead!"

He came rushing out the kitchen door, and we both ran to the studio. It seemed like we were running in slow motion, and I can still see the look on Scott's face.

I would need my husband that day as never before. I had failed at marriage long before I met Grant's dad, humbly asking forgiveness for my part in it. I didn't want another divorce, yet it happened again when Grant was five. The differences between Grant's dad and me grew stronger, and I couldn't convince him to keep trying to resolve them. We stayed on friendly terms to soften the blow for our son's sake.

As time passed, Grant adjusted to the changes and seemed to accept them, often asking if I would marry again. His dad had remarried, and he wanted me to be happy, too.

For good reason, I didn't trust my choices in marriage so it was unlikely. Was there a godly man who would forgive and understand my history and love us both? Four years passed as I worked and raised my son—and then prayers were answered as I was blessed with another chance. My son was excited and a little nervous about moving and starting over. Scott, true to his promise, was always as good to Grant as he is to his own children and grandchildren.

I can still hear 9-year-old Grant crowing to his Sedan friends, "My new dad Scott lives in Fort Scott and used to live on Scott Street!" He thought the coincidence was almost magical.

I wanted to go back to that moment, to any moment, as we rushed to our son's side and stood over him. His second dad for almost 17 years called his name as he reached for Grant's wrist.

He was shaking as he repeated, "No...oh, no..."

I kept crying out, "My baby!"

Scott somehow composed himself and went on automatic, dialing 911 as I called Grant's dad in Oklahoma. I recounted, in quiet hysteria, what we had just discovered as he listened in stunned silence. The rest of the afternoon was surreal. The police arrived, EMTs came, and later, the local mortician who had grown up with my husband showed up. I also messaged the fiancée of Grant's best friend. The two of them arrived, only to watch in disbelief as the scene played out, complete with an investigation that wouldn't be over until the mandatory autopsy was completed.

The detective, a kindly middle-aged man, was calm and professional as he said, "We have to pursue this case because your son passed away alone, at a young age, with no known history of life-threatening health conditions."

The officers went through Grant's luggage, truck, and every square foot of the studio as we sat in our kitchen and answered questions. Then, we were given one last chance to view Grant before he was taken away. I gazed at him and stroked his hair, whispering, *"My son...my son..."* as an officer stood at the door and politely looked away. What a strange moment it was! My own heart felt as if it had stopped beating, too.

Somehow, I continued breathing. I had to function. Scott and I talked in circles, discussing cremation and final arrangements, and then spent a sleepless night as I shook in his arms. The next day was filled with emotional phone calls to family and friends. Then, I began the solemn task of writing my son's obituary. I alternated between feeling numb and being devastated, but the words came easily. My emotions were overflowing with the essence of who Grant was and is and all that he means to me.

Grant valued his friends and cared about people from all walks of life. He was the kind of guy who would help with chores, cook for you, give you his last dollar, listen to your problems, open doors for a lady, and change tires for a stranger. He loved the outdoors, hunting, fishing, camping, and had also been an excellent athlete who played a variety of sports. Rodeo was something that he particularly enjoyed, and he entered rough events that made me uneasy.

He used to joke, "Mom, you'd cover me in bubble wrap if you could."

I didn't realize how many others had experienced his humor and kindness until the responses started flooding his Facebook page. Then, the messages and cards began to arrive along with beautiful plants and flowers. It comforted me in some kind of deep, needy way. It was important to know that people cared, that my son's life had meaning, that his goodness was recognized, and that his passing was truly mourned.

Although Grant and I attended local church services as he grew up, he was quite young when I was led to join a non-denominational church in the Ozarks that provided deeper study. Because of this, my Christian family is scattered for the most part although I'm grateful for their long-distance support, as well as for the support of others from different chapters in my life. Grant's caring array of closest friends, in particular, helped to sustain me. It showed me how much he was loved and appreciated during his time here. I really had no idea how many lives he had affected until his death.

He was mischievous at times, naive and foolish at others, but always a loving and gentle soul. One of my favorite memories of Grant happened when my mother passed away in 2004. He was 11 years old and rode his bike to the local drug store to buy a condolence card with his allowance. He wrote, *"She is in a better place, with no pain."* I keep it in a special place.

He really was a good kid, but like the rest of us, far from perfect. He had a couple of incidents in his later teens that created some legal problems, with a DUI being the most serious. It was a country road incident after spending the day with friends at a Missouri lake—an incident that he regretted and would never repeat. I thanked God that no one was hurt and life went on.

I know that Grant had good moments and enjoyable times along the way, but he also encountered more than his share of disappointments. I wanted to help him and tried in many ways, hoping to change things for the better and comfort him as I did when he was younger. But I couldn't.

He became disillusioned as he moved into his twenties. I can still hear him saying, "Maybe I should be a jerk. Nobody wants Mr. Nice Guy, except for a friend, of course."

"Son, there are lots of nice, young women out there. Are you looking for the wrong kind, in the wrong places? Inner beauty is the most important."

"I have to be attracted to them, Mom. It's not going to happen, anyway."

"Just don't do something you'll regret, trying to fill a void in your life."

"You have no idea how many voids are in my life."

And so it went. After he passed, a lovely young woman surfaced who had deep feelings for him and had known him for years. She told me her big regret was not telling him how she really felt. We've become close, and now I'm praying that someone special enters her life, too, just as I used to pray for Grant.

I thought of my many prayers as we decorated a large table for his visitation, filled with pictures, sports trophies, his cowboy hat and boots, Indian artifacts that he found growing up on Buck Creek—one of his favorite caps and sunglasses—lots of little things that meant something to him, with two huge vases of flowers towering above it all.

His celebration of life had a big turnout, with some faces I didn't recognize. They introduced themselves and consoled me with kind words that faded as they said them. Grant's Oklahoma family joined us, too, for hugs, tears and the sharing of memories. A gathering was held afterward at a local pizza place, serving some of Grant's favorite foods as the reminiscing continued.

The actual memorial service, held the next day in Copan, Oklahoma, was arranged by Grant's dad, second mom, and his sister by marriage. Many of their close friends provided for it, and it was more of the same, on a grander scale. It was held at Grant's high school gymnasium with standing room only. It thrilled me and broke my heart at the same time. When I saw the memorial video play, with his smiling face flashing by to country music, it almost felt like an out-of-body experience.

Weeks went by as we waited for the initial results of the autopsy. I followed a list of things to do that would tie up loose ends, including more notifications and some legal correspondence.

I also kept checking his obituary because the views were growing at an incredible rate. The last time I looked, and I've probably gone in around 20 times, total views were up to 11,760. We live in a small town of 8,000. Grant left here after his sophomore year although he had local friends he stayed in touch with. I wondered if his closest friends were running the numbers up as a sort of tribute, another sad, sweet thing for me to ponder.

I started going through old photos, and we had a couple of them enlarged and framed: our last Christmas together in 2018 and my favorite mom-and-son picture from our trip to Claremore for a final follow up after Grant's foot surgery from an old sports injury. In the latter, we were celebrating Grant's release at the Will Rogers Museum.

I continually look back on our family vacations, holidays, celebrations and milestones. There is so much to remember as I sit here wondering about the countless other parents who are also left with only memories. I hope they have the comfort of faith, knowing that we will all be reunited someday in God's perfect timing. I realize that there are families out there who wonder if their loved one made it to Paradise and perhaps still agonize over not knowing. This is why I'm going to share information that I didn't want made public, not at first. After praying about it, I hope that it will comfort others and reassure them that our Father in heaven is filled with more compassion and grace than we can possibly grasp.

The preliminary autopsy stated that Grant had died of a cocaine overdose. When the detective shared this with us, I couldn't accept it. Grant hadn't displayed any of the reactions of someone on a cocaine high. I didn't know that he had ever used it. I immediately started making excuses. I thought that it must have been a recent thing, that he was so attached to his contractor friends that he let some of them entice him into trying it. Actually, I still think that. Being on the road can be lonely and boring. Then, my mind raced to the fact that he had spent a couple of nights with one of his contractor friends who lives a few miles from our house. I realized that he was gone that last night, too, for a while, and that we didn't start our visit until around 10 pm. It came to mind again how secretly unhappy he had been.

The detective was very gentle. He said that it was just a preliminary report and the cause of death could be something else entirely. I tried to diminish it somehow, recalling my own history as a young woman. I had experimented a little, too, although I had long ago repented of those moments. I've heard rumors of prominent individuals in our community who have drug dealers on call and personally know of a teacher who did drugs in a different community and an attorney, too. It does go on. It isn't right, but it happens, with every kind of person, and all over the world.

My mind drifted to the issue of legalized marijuana, a topic that Grant and I had discussed more than once. He was convinced of its medicinal value, which I had to admit exists, but I insisted that it needs to be in the form of CBD oil, reminding him that marijuana is illegal in many states. I remembered his younger years, when he was completely against using marijuana. I shared some of my own youthful mistakes with him in the hope that he would use good judgement and not give in to peer pressure. The subject was always dropped without resolution, and my prayers continued that he would grow as a Christian and trust God with his life.

I kept thinking about the moment when I anointed Grant for healing, and I cried out to God for a sign that Grant had been forgiven and taken to Heaven. Father took pity on me. I received profound messages and signs over a 4-month period, as his ashes were scattered in two different places.

I chose to keep a small silver container with some of his ashes for myself. It rests at the foot of a cross on my cabinet, near his picture. I look at it often, as I remember the beautiful, supernatural signs that my son is indeed in Paradise. Each one is a treasure, recorded in my Bible, and I vividly recall them every time my sadness starts to overcome me.

I had already received three signs by the time the final police investigation results were in, which helped to absorb the shock that Grant had died from cardiomegaly—an enlarged heart—combined with cocaine usage. The evidence of a spider bite was noted but not clearly defined as a contributing factor. Again, my mind went around and around the facts. Had Grant's heart been damaged in sports? He had mentioned a sharp pain near his heart after the spider bite. Did the poison bring it on? Did he take too much cocaine at a different time, or shortly before he passed? So many unanswered questions! My dear Grant, with a huge heart for everyone all of his life. It almost seemed ironic to me, and it was almost too much for me to bear—except the signs kept appearing that all was well.

I want to share the messages and signs that I have been blessed with, but it's important to me that anyone reading this understand that our God is no respecter of persons and that He loves all of His children. I'm hardly an example of the model person, and I'm confessing it here. Yet, He has blessed and comforted me beyond anything I could have hoped for.

When He forgives, it is truly gone even if the world never lets you forget.

I've heard of many others receiving signs of comfort, and then there are those who haven't. I don't pretend to know why. Possibly, it's a matter of faith. Or maybe those individuals aren't ready for some reason. Maybe their signs will arrive later, or perhaps they will simply and beautifully be blessed with a great sense of peace concerning their loved ones.

For me, it was imperative to somehow know, and so prayers were fervently said. There have been other supernatural moments in my life, at different times, for different reasons, but these signs were like no other moment in my life. Father began giving me what I needed.

I was reading Psalm 23 a few nights after my son was gone and felt led to pull a bookmark out from somewhere in the middle of my Bible. Grant had given it to me and written a note on the back of it, telling me that he would love me forever as his mother. The word *forever* stood out to me and held my gaze. Our motto, as with many families, had been "Always and Forever, No Matter What." We wrote it to each other often in notes and cards over the years.

My eyes were then drawn to the final line of the psalm, *I will dwell in the house of the Lord forever*. A deep, comforting feeling came over me. I knew that it was a message from my son. I held the bookmark, closely, for quite some time that night.

A week later, a close friend of Grant's messaged me about a dream she had the night before. Grant was smiling in the clouds as she looked up. His Oklahoma memorial had just taken place, and I had comforted another dear friend of his on the same night, telling her that he was smiling in the heavenly places, and she had to keep her beautiful smile, too.

The timing of the dream and my declaration were purposed. I knew it, instantly.

A few days later, my husband and I were preparing to eat dinner at the kitchen table. I was trying to act normal although a sort of quiet shock surrounded me in my daily life. We held hands and gave thanks.

I asked Father to bless and cleanse, then added, "Thank You for keeping Grant safe in Heaven."

I immediately felt compelled to turn to the right of the room and look at a plaque that hangs near the doorway. It has our motto inscribed on it. The word *forever*, written in a brownish copper color, was literally shining in gold, lifted off of the wall. It was a soft, golden light that remained suspended for several seconds. I couldn't make a sound. It was stunning. Scott was facing the opposite direction and was oblivious to what was happening. I looked around as if to see a logical reason for it, but there was no logical reason. I knew that I was being given a wonderful sign.

Later, I asked Father to specifically speak to me through His Word concerning Grant. I opened my Bible and was taken to Psalm 138—with an immediate inner knowledge that something important was about to happen. Then, there it was—Psalm 138:8. At some point in time, I had circled it and written *My Grant* within the circle. It read; *The Lord will perfect that which concerns me.*

I know that God does not make mistakes. He could have chosen to intervene in my son's life in a way which would have stopped him from making a fatal choice. Others have had their lives turned around and set upon good paths. Others have been brought back from the brink of death because the Lord has other plans for them here. Yet, Father decided to take my son home, which is sometimes the ultimate healing and sometimes, done for the greater good.

It is written in 1 Peter 4:8 that love covers a multitude of sins—and Grant has great love. It is written in Proverbs 21:2 that the LORD weighs our hearts. He is the heart knower. Grant, in his final moments, perhaps in his last second of fleshly life, must have reached out to Jesus. His spirit would have known to do that. I also believe that the anointing enveloped forgiveness as well. My sorrow and grief have been tempered by my sure faith in Father's goodness and in a greater plan that I must trust in as I lean not unto my own understanding.

I now believe, with surety, that Grant's final return home was purposed. We were given some extra time together that I cherish although I wish there had been more. Don't we always wish for more when our plans are stopped and life changes forever? What we shared included two of my old poems, which he had never read before. One of them was published in *Home Life* three years before I knew I would have a baby late in life, with mixed feelings that included an underlying uneasiness that something could go wrong. The poem spoke of tenderness and trials and of happiness, too.

Grant seemed to find it sobering. "Mom, it gave me chills."

This is what he read. To me, it almost seems prophetic.

LOVELY CHILD OF MINE

I look at you with pleasure
as I touch your skin of silk—
head upon my resting arm
drinking of my milk.
Your laughter is my comfort,
your smile, it greets my own.
You reach for me, and in your need
I find my heart has grown.

In simple things you feel a joy
I pray these years will not destroy.
The innocence your eyes reveal—
the wonderment you make so real.
You, my love, are rich with life
and though your hurt will be a knife
that slices through this heart of mine
when disappointments form,
I pray that I can help you
when life begins its storm.
And storm it will, my little one.
You'll feel the pain draw near,
the loss of love that churns and aches,
the taste of sorrowful tears.
How well I know—
I'm ready.
God will help us when it's time.
For now, I marvel at my prize,
lovely child of mine.

We lapsed into silence. I felt there was something else
that he wanted to tell me, but he didn't. We continued to look
at each other, in a way we never had before, until he finally
broke eye contact and the mood changed. My mind goes to
that moment often as the months move along.

I began sorting through his belongings, trying to decide
what to keep. Grant loved clothes, and we decided to donate
part of them to a free clothing organization in town. He also
had boxes and drawers filled with sports gear, collectables
and miscellaneous although certain items were missing. He
was known to loan things out, give them away, and leave
belongings scattered from one place to the next.

His dad in Oklahoma asked if his silver spurs were in
the studio—the main item he hoped to receive as a keepsake.

They had been custom made for Grant by his uncle, with his name engraved on the inside of one spur and his initials on the other. They were missing though, and no one seemed to know where they ended up.

Then, we received a call from our sales rep at the local car dealership. We had worked it out with him to return Grant's truck because it was the best option under the circumstances. It turned out that he's a collector of western memorabilia and had recently purchased the spurs through a sale, not connecting the name immediately with who the owner had been. Scott has known and worked with him on other car deals for years. His reputation and ethics are excellent, and we knew that we had personally emptied the truck of all of Grant's belongings.

He kindly returned the spurs to us that day, knowing what they meant to us—just as I knew that such a well-timed discovery from a local individual who had a number to contact us was seemingly impossible and had the hand of God mightily upon it. What I may never know is how it ended up in a sale or why. Our God works in mysterious ways, and I wonder if Grant asked Him to arrange it, to comfort his dad and provide yet another sign that all is well.

It was later decided that the majority of Grant's ashes would be released at Buck Creek in Osage County, Oklahoma, where we had lived as a family until he turned five and where he had hoped to return someday to establish his own home. Before moving back with his dad, he had returned there for rotating weekends, holidays, and summers, where his love of nature and the cowboy way of life would become ingrained into his being.

We took our son home, just as he would have wanted, joining his dad and stepmother on a beautiful autumn day in October. Along with his ashes, we brought Psalm 23 to read as his remains were released into the bubbling creek, fall flowers to send down the stream in his honor, and mementos that I knew his dad would want to keep, including the much-prized silver spurs.

They, in turn, gave me Grant's childhood Bible with his name engraved on the front cover. He had received it while attending a country church with them years ago. Inside was a photo of him smiling as a shepherd boy at the altar, standing with a group of children portraying characters in the nativity scene as the cross of Jesus stood out in the background. I could see God's love on each of their faces.

The Lord was with us that day, too, and I had asked for our son to be present in spirit. The ceremony was simple and very moving. Afterward, we collected rocks from the bank to place in my memory garden at home. Everyone searched with me for a variety of river rock and slate, gathering different sizes, colors, and shapes for my own mementos. I hoped above all to find one that was heart-shaped—amd there it was, at my feet!

The moment I saw it, a picture flashed into my mind of a photo that I have of myself and five-year old Grant. We are giving each other an affectionate touch, nose to nose. It's a profile picture, taken at a fall festival shortly after the two of us moved from the ranch to nearby Sedan, Kansas. It hangs on our Christmas tree each year in a holiday frame, an irreplaceable memory.

I picked the heart-shaped rock up and immediately saw that it was etched in an incredible way. The profile of myself and Grant, giving each other an "Eskimo kiss" was obvious. It was primitive, but undeniable. Again, I felt stunned and wasn't able to fully process the miracle until later. My gratitude and sorrow became one.

"Thank you, Father, again and again…"

Two weeks later, an old friend and I took Grant's remaining ashes to Eureka Springs, Arkansas, my favorite place for

Autumn retreats. Scott stayed home to care for our animals and give me a chance to fulfill my final mission with a much needed break during my most loved season of the year.

There was a light, misty rain at times, but the weekend was still lovely. I tried to take momentary breaks from my thoughts of Grant as we enjoyed the hills, foliage and turn of the century charm that's unique and family oriented.

On our final day, we went to Inspiration Point, a gorgeous outlook that gives a sweeping view of the valley below. In years past, I've looked upon multi-colored trees scattered among streams, farm houses and red roofed barns, all of it appearing miniature from the fenced area above. It was always breathtaking in the sunlight, but that morning, it was cloudy with patches of fog as we drove up the winding road to our destination. I clutched my small pouch of ashes and asked to be alone for a moment to pray and reflect. No one else was there, which was very unusual.

I approached the observation area and looked down. The entire valley was filled with fog that completely blanketed the view. It literally reached up to right below the fence where I stood. At first, I wondered if I should return later, but something held me there. As I continued to look at the thick cover of fog, a small, circular rainbow, in a soft lavender color, began forming, directly below me, hovering on top of the fog. I was mesmerized and didn't move. As I continued to look, my shadow was projected into the center of it.

There was no sun that day, and there was no rational way that it could be happening. It could only have been the light of God, and there are no words to fully describe its beauty. I called out to my friend to join me, wondering if she'd be able to see it too. She looked down and her breath drew in.

"Oh Marti, Marti."

We continued to gaze at it, as my beautiful gift, my rainbow, slowly began to disappear. As it did, I released Grant's ashes. Part of them fell into the fog, part remained on the rocks directly below the fence. We went to the car without speaking, as I tried to regain my composure enough to drive. I had asked Father for Grant's spirit to be with us that day, too, and it was so spectacular that I was in awe. I will remain in awe for the rest of my earthly life.

Thorncrown Chapel was our next destination, which we had passed on our way. It's a stunning, all glass, non-denominational church nestled in the hills. Visitors come for Sunday services, weddings, or just to sit in its sanctuary and be inspired by the magnificence of the architecture and the surrounding beauty from all sides. As we approached it, walking up the stone path to the entrance, I heard an angelic voice singing. We entered and sat down as he continued to play the piano and minister in song.

He was performing, *It Is Well With My Soul.* As soon as I grasped the lyrics, I knew without doubt that it was a message from Grant. As he finished the selection, he immediately began singing *I Can Only Imagine,* which is one of the songs I had already chosen for my personal memory video. Again, it washed over me. How astounding it must have been for my son to come face to face with his Lord and Savior. What a brilliant, unspeakably glorious moment it must have been.

I believed the events that day were most likely the grand finale of Father's great and gracious comforts. But there was one more thing to come. While I was pregnant with Grant, I went to a Christian counselor for help with my troubled marriage. Prior to that, I'd decided not to have testing done on my unborn baby, not even to learn of the sex. I was taking a leap of faith and trusting God for the outcome.

The counselor was aware that I made the appointment concerning personal problems—yet after our initial greeting, she immediately declared a prophesy over my unborn child.

She said, "Your son will be a lover of mankind and a leader of men."

She called the baby 'my son' in her astounding announcement. I was amazed, and after our session, I returned home and wrote what she said in my newly purchased baby book. I thought to myself, *time will tell*.

Grant was certainly a lover of mankind—this became even more evident after his passing. That part of the prophesy was absolutely true. Was it possible that Father would use Grant in His heavenly army, allowing him to be one of the leaders? It would be the only way that the full prophesy could now become fulfilled. I reminded myself that Grant had been forgiven, was now in heaven, and that it was all a matter of God's will for a portion of his eternal life.

Then came a phone call on April 5, 2020. A Christian friend and I began to talk about Grant, about how wonderful his heavenly life must be. There was a pause and she said that something was happening. She started describing a vision that she was being given about him—describing it to me as it was happening, under the unction of the Holy Spirit.

Grant was leading a large group of heavenly soldiers on horseback, all in full uniform, white with touches of red. Their helmets were shining, and their horses were moving in perfect sync with each other as they galloped among the clouds. She stated that Grant was sitting tall and erect, looking straight ahead, as were the other soldiers, with the winds blowing over them as they moved in perfect formation. They were on a mission, with Christ invisibly guiding them all. I was overcome with emotion and began to cry. This would make the full prophesy come true, and I have a feeling that I will see it someday—and I now wait with much anticipation.

All of this has given my heart great comfort as I continue my journey here on earth, with each of the precious gifts I've shared lifting me from what would have been a dark place of despair. Our Father, who knows and sees all, must have realized that I would need them to carry on, and that I would share them with others.

And how could I forget them, (in contrast to my flawed history—which is not remembered by Father, just as the details of my son's passing are completely erased in His eyes, in showing, yet again the everlasting and abounding love of our LORD)!

For many of us, there is no way of knowing the last thoughts of our loved ones, or what transpired in the final moments before they passed, but our God is the very definition of love, and I believe that one Word, one Name, uttered silently or aloud, would be enough.

I hope and pray that anyone needing a heavenly sign, or a divine touch, will ask in faith, and believe that you will receive what you seek—that you may also be comforted and continue on in a way that honors both God and your loved one's memory…

And now I speak to Grant. I will miss you, my son, for the rest of my earthly life. Yet it is eased in knowing that Father God has a great plan in effect, and His mercy and grace are far greater than we comprehend. I quote in part from Ecclesiastes 3:

"For everything there is a season, and a time for every matter under heaven: a time to be born, and a time to die; a time to weep, and a time to laugh; a time to mourn, and a time to dance."

I believe that you now dance with joy in heaven and ride upon the clouds, enjoying immense beauty as you praise and serve our Lord—for Father has made it overwhelmingly clear that Jesus forgave you and removed, *forever*, all of your pain and secret sorrows.

We shall enjoy each other again, dear Grant, in God's perfect timing and will. Yes, my mother's heart does weep, but my spirit rejoices that you now have eternal life, with peace and happiness beyond compare. As I remember your day of birth with great love, I acknowledge the words of *Ecclesiastes* 7 to be true. Your day of death is the greater of the two.

2 Corinthians 5:8 Yes, we do have confidence, and we would rather be away from the body and at home with the Lord.

COMFORT

I was embraced that day, in the abyss of your absence. Familiar faces moving close, in a scattered line—for a gathering of sympathy, a remembrance of life. Such a sweet, caring son. Gone far too soon. *Oh yes, thank you.* How very well I knew.

The room filled with murmurings, as I drew back and stepped aside. Shock, with a caring sweep, took much of what I felt—and kept it for a while. I welcomed it to stay, for as long as I might need. Then the release, just a little at a time, with the most outstanding moments I could find. With the slightest sound, the smallest of a shout, it released its hold and more of what I lost came pouring out.

Lord, may I be drenched in kindness. Let it cover me completely. And some souls I know still reach out in unexpected ways, while others have moved on, silently. Isn't that the way it goes? At least it has for me. Lord, I don't understand. But I pray for Your peace...

As I look back upon the years, your arrival and your departure, too, I know that nothing in this world of flesh and blood is destined to remain. Still, I am embraced by your memory, by all that it makes me feel. And I learn, with each passing day, that the comfort of God is real.

Psalm 34:18 The LORD is near to the brokenhearted, and saves the crushed in spirit.

SPOTS OF SPLENDOR

We traveled often to find them,
didn't we, my boy,
those places of beauty that lay
upon the land itself.
That would engulf us with joy,
lifting us from a common day
with an array of Godly pleasures.
We would walk the tall grasses,
cool and green in a prairie spring,
to the creek, rippling on rock ledges,
heaped with flint and slate, spilled
upon the water's edge.
The woods, with its thick floor
of fallen leaves and brittle twigs
became our walking path—
where coyotes and hawks were hiding,
where morels grew fat for frying
and arrowheads surfaced in red clay.
An Oklahoma afternoon, with
wild onion bouquets and fish for the catching.
Such spots of splendor, not a mile away,
ours, for as long as we stayed.

Psalm 16:11 You show me the path of life. In your presence there is fullness of joy; in your right hand are pleasures forevermore.

COLORS OF A DIFFERENT WORLD

I think of Heaven today. And you in it. I consider the beginning of greatness, when God chose to envision and fully create; His miraculous power that brought it to pass—such endless, flawless beauty. A land of perfection, stellar to behold. A creation that springs from majesty. We find a portion here, given of God for all to see. But there, it is far beyond what our earthly senses can perceive. A paradise, pure and serene, soaring with light and grand beyond measure. An eternity filled with indescribable treasure, for those who have truly believed.

And there you are, somewhere near His throne, or traveling the universe at His divine command. Your smile glows, dazzled by the colors of a different world, amid recollections from long ago. There is a time to worship, a time to reflect—moments to share with countless other souls, who gladly partake. I guess at the pleasures offered, each of them blissful, each profound. Rewards that grace you again and again—such moments to abound…

There are no words, really, for what it must be. I will delve further, silently—as I think of Heaven today, and you in it.

1 Corinthians 2:9 But, as it is written, "What no eye has seen, nor ear heard, nor the human heart conceived, what God has prepared for those who love him."

THE GARDENS OF GOD

There will be delight in the choosing,
as we make our way between
heaven's remarkable scenes.
Together, arm in arm, with
the walking paths themselves, a work of peace.
I see a stately bench in my imaginings,
elaborately carved—Welcome, it says
to all who pass by.
We shall sit there often,
near The River of Life.
I have long awaited questions for you,
as we take our rest,
and many things to tell you, too.

Psalm 23:1-2 The LORD is my shepherd, I shall not want.
He makes me lie down in green pastures; He leads me beside
still waters.

THE LOVELY THINGS

Today, I look fondly upon this place, this life of mine, in a softer way, from a different view. Choosing to see something new, even in its long-lived state. To peer upon my world and see the faintest lovely things grow large, as the smallest acts of kindness show their power.

Weary of grief, this choice was made. A call for beauty among ashes, overlooked before, pulled from a time that cannot return, from thoughts that churned in an aching stream. Those were the days when I dwelled on my loss—when it seemed there was nothing more.

But there is always more. "God, help me," I said, "to seek them out, the parts that will cover the rest of my life." Shaping the corners where you once stood, connecting the spaces that you once filled, I asked for something to move me when I stand too still. And faith came upon me. It carried me along, and I went with it, willingly.

I now study what goodness remains. I linger upon it daily—for it is the goodness that I must always keep in sight. This is how I look fondly upon this place, this life that is now mine.

Philippians 4:8 Whatever is true, whatever is honorable... whatever is pleasing...if there is anything worthy of praise, think about these things.

Marti Wells-Smith

CLOUDS IN A BLUE SKY

Who could phantom it,
all that we saw,
all that surrounded us.
We looked up
to clouds in a blue sky,
shaped, sculpted,
curled and white—
they moved slowly at times,
with elegance.
And there we were,
two wondering souls,
standing small and in awe of God,
together, down below.
The water's reflection a marvel,
greens mixed with shimmered blue
and shots of white gold beaming—
with tree boughs leaning in
and waving with the wind.
We watched it intently
until the day's end,
until the memory was made...
I recollect so clearly
as I look again, today.

Psalm 104:31 May the glory of the LORD endure forever;
may the LORD rejoice in his works...

SEVEN MONTHS TODAY

The passing of time is silent, as it carries your face, your smile. It moves one minute, then another, without a glance at the hours gone by. It shifts through my life and stops at nothing, second by second, moving through—and it is what God has instructed time to do.

While I wait here, on the outskirts—the mother of memories...to catch a glimpse of you, as it moves us both along. And for that moment, you have returned, as if you were never gone.

Knowing there is more to come, I trust, as I recall. For there is no goodbye when faith moves, too, stronger than it all. It is seven months today, and God knows I will wait. Until then, until the end of time—I, too, will carry your smile next to mine.

Philippians 1:3 I thank my God every time I remember you...

Marti Wells-Smith

THE REST OF OUR JOURNEY

We are fashioned and formed
by what works upon us;
much like the cliffs, gouged beautifully,
as great waters
pulse their waves and slam debris.
Life cuts an image, and deep.
We move at a chosen pace
or toss about in winds of the unknown,
torrentially, or at ease.
We wade out, arms swaying, into the deep,
and only then, realize where we are.
And only then, for many,
in a loss bigger than the sea,
will we search for clefts,
and rise upon the Rock,
to hold fast for the rest of our journey.

Psalm 18:2 The Lord is my rock, my fortress and my deliverer, my God, my rock in whom I take refuge, my shield and the horn of my salvation, my stronghold.

DRIVING IN THE DARK

To drive with eyes closed, on an empty road, not caring if bridge and ditch were hit with force, to go over a cliff, or plunge into the mountainside, or merely go screaming into the night. These were troubled thoughts of mine, when the ache would begin to jump inside, with the mightiest of weights.

Before the waking moment, when mind and body rest as one, there was a lapse of knowing, a forgetfulness—a hollowed out reprieve. I found a short, harmless escape, within the deepest sleep.

Yet, I was a woman of faith, who knew of the struggle that it would take to arrive at a peaceful place. I prayed for God to relieve my plight, and the despairing thoughts did fade...

And how many of us, here and everywhere, have traveled this unwanted road, as each of us head to our eternal home?

Jeremiah 17:14 Heal me, O LORD, and I shall be healed; save me and I shall be saved; for You are my praise.

GETTING THROUGH IT

Breakfast is coffee and a pill.
Lunch, a leftover, if there are any.
My husband, a considerate soul,
leaves, to give me solitude—
for I choose to remain alone.
My pets need me, of course,
and I attend to them dutifully.
I remember to brush my teeth
sometime after 3,
and then retreat to the porch.
Windows are open to the breeze
as I sit, still in my night clothes—
pondering in disjointed prayer.
I think of all that my son offered,
if only he could have stayed.
I open my mouth to moan and wail.
Then a sip of tea,
and then the rest of the day…

John 16:22 So you have pain now; but I will see you again, and your hearts will rejoice, and no one will take your joy from you.

THE SAVORING

The day suspends, as I pretend you are here—here again, with me. My recollections bounce and blend, from one year to the next. Just look at you, a timid crawl, your first step soon, then running! Look at us, we're at the park, and aren't we having fun.

I sang lullabies and held you close, when I was the one you wanted most and life was a simpler time…The phone rings, and rings again. I ignore it until it finally ends. I think of your dreams and all that life seemed, as I take you to age nine—where life hadn't cut you too deeply yet, and we shared no large regrets.

A truck huffs by, then a slammed-on brake. Wincing, I review our prairie days. You were three—no, four—the year of your favorite dinosaur cake. There would be 21 more, then, no others. I sit here, savoring all but the loss of you, a woman who doesn't know what to do.

Faith, take me to God's throne, where I will ask for help…and where I won't feel so alone.

Psalm 25:16 Turn to me and be gracious to me, for I am lonely and afflicted.

Marti Wells-Smith

VOICES FROM ANOTHER ROOM

The walls are thin at times,
muffled sounds come through;
words, in pieces, filter in
from voices in another room.
The sounds at my door grow loud,
I hear my name and strain for more—
my tragedy in detail—
the topic of the night.
I peek upon their pity,
almost dripping in my sight.
Such a loss, but Heaven's gain,
I will explode if I hear it said again.
The relatives are gathered
in a loving show.
I hide behind the darkened walls,
and wait for them to go.

Psalm 31:9 Be gracious to me, O Lord, for I am in distress;
my eye wastes away from grief, my soul and body also.

THE GOODNESS OF IT

I rise up to a new day, in faith,
as sunlight stands at the window
looking in.
It enters, small poles of light
inviting me outside;
where it takes the air and
surrounds it, loosely—
that all around may breathe it,
and feel its heated rays as one.
Arched in the blue and white of morning—
the goodness of it surrounds the sky,
as it diminishes the woeful thoughts
that entered my mind last night.

Romans 15:13 May the God of hope fill you with all joy and peace in believing, so that you may abound in hope by the power of the Holy Spirit.

Marti Wells-Smith

GOING ELSEWHERE

Lord, let me step away
from the battle of grief—
and the energy spent to heal.
I need to escape; I ask to retreat.
Just for now,
to other parts of my life,
to other thoughts, recollections,
separate from my loss.
Perhaps little else
will cross my mind,
of that, I can't be sure.
But I feel a stirring, Lord.
Please bless me with the words.

Proverbs 27:19 Just as water reflects the face, so one human heart reflects another.

THINGS TO REMEMBER
THINGS TO FORGET

Marti Wells-Smith

FROM LONG AGO

I'm reviewing some of my life tonight, with soft lights and Sirius XM in the background. So much has happened, particularly this past year, that I want to reach back and take another look. My first memory is one that happened when I was only two years old. I remember seeing mom right outside the front door, watering shrubs. I went to the kitchen and took two spoons out of the drawer and gave one to my baby brother, who was a year younger. He followed my lead and helped me dig the dirt out of a philodendron plant on the coffee table. Perhaps I thought it was something fun to do—that part I don't remember.

Mom walked in, saw the piled dirt on the table and didn't say a word. My brother and I looked back at her as we dangled the spoons, maybe smiling, but I'm not sure. She then ran to her bedroom and threw herself face first on her bed and started sobbing. I see myself walking to the side of the bed and just standing there, feeling terrible. I had made my mama cry, and it wouldn't be the only time. It's the first time I remember hurting someone.

From there, it's a blur until kindergarten, with two unrelated memories—walking hand in hand with an aunt, and taking a nap with the other little kids on our roll-up pallets. In-between, it was typical small-town life, with my recollections sustained, in great part, by the 8-millimeter films that Dad shot every holiday.

Then came first grade, and it was painful. We lived across the street from the elementary school, and I dreaded crossing it to face the mean, sour-faced Miss Coker (not her real name, of course). I found out, eventually, that she always chose a student to pick on, and I was the unlucky one that year. She would ignore me when my hand was raised, and I literally peed my pants once because she wouldn't let me go to the bathroom.

But that's minor compared to the morning when a softball popped me in the face at recess. My eye was throbbing, swollen twice its size and turning purple. When class resumed, she ignored my raised hand, as always. At the afternoon recess, I ran home for help—where my mom iced my eye before walking me back to confront her.

Miss Coker said, "I didn't realize she was hurting...blah, blah."

After Mom left, she grabbed me in front of the other students and shook me hard as she told me that I must never leave the premises again to get my parents. I was mortified. She began mistreating me even more that day. I was the tallest in my class, not a petite six-year-old in any way—just a nice child, who was made to sit in the hallway as punishment for coughing too hard, or accidently dropping my pencil. Any little thing would do. I was set aside and marked. I would break out in rebellion during my high school years—to try and prove that I was worthy. My parents, bless their hearts, didn't know what to do about it, so they just hoped for the best. That's my first memory of someone hurting me.

I became a studious bookworm and dreamer, surviving first grade and moving on with relief. In third grade, I won a prize in Sunday school for memorizing the most scriptures. I received a picture of Jesus that glowed in the dark and was very proud of it—hanging it on my bedroom wall, where I could see it at night and feel comforted when it was stormy outside.

That was the year that I befriended a sweet girl in my class with learning disabilities. "Tina" would wrap her arm around her notebook paper as she worked on her lessons, trying to hide the fact that she couldn't write. I peeked once, and she was scribbling lines with her pencil. I understood what it felt like to be an outsider and invited her home, where I created a makeshift school. I tried to make her feel welcome as I taught her the alphabet and how to make a few, simple words.

She was delighted to have a friend, and really tried to learn. But the next time we played, she couldn't remember any of it, and eventually, I stopped trying. Meanwhile, she was moved from grade to grade until she dropped out before entering high school. Special Education didn't exist in our town at that time; children with learning disabilities became casualties.

Many years later, her husband brought a letter to my mom that he had written on her behalf. It was addressed to me. It said that Tina had never forgotten my kindness and thought of me often. It was humbling and sad—and made me wish that I had done more for her. Judging by the letter, it seemed that she had found a nice guy who was helping her through life. I hope so. This is my first recollection of an entire system hurting someone.

My fifth-grade year was the summer of backyard plays—with productions that I directed and appeared in, charging a penny a show just to get some neighborhood kids to attend. My secret crush, "Joey," was the co-star. He lived across the street and also played army with my two brothers, allowing me to be the battalion nurse when they were wounded in crossfire.

He was a cute guy, and I swooned as we rehearsed for all of five minutes until showtime. I recited poetry and sang and danced a little, and he was the standup comic, with a string of knock-knock jokes as his grand finale.

Joey moved away before school started again. It was the first time that my heart was broken. I heard that he married after graduation and joined the military for real. It was hard to lose my special friend, and I've wanted to send him a letter, too, more than once.

Freshman year, I started to blossom and life changed for the better. I was rebellious, but not terribly so, just enough to try and grow up too fast. There were good times and some fun experiences as I dated, enjoyed the arts, and in particular, was the editor of our school paper. But I was always that dorky, unpopular little girl deep inside—the one who wore practical shoes and was kind of chubby and embarrassed.

My senior year was a lesson all its own. A month before we graduated, our journalism teacher —I'll call her "Miss White"—was fired, and one of our classmates was expelled concerning rumors of inappropriate behavior. I really liked her and the classmate was a nice guy who was shy and awkward, an unlikely candidate for anything seriously unacceptable. I was called into the superintendent's office and questioned, probably because they knew I was involved in her classes.

"I really don't know anything—this is all news to me."

She was fired, nonetheless. I didn't believe it happened, and none of her other students did either. I wanted the chance to tell her how I felt, but she immediately left town and I didn't see her again—until my freshman year at nearby Pitt State. She came into the restaurant where I was working and glared at me when I tried to wait on her.

"It's good to see you."

"I don't know why."

Her expression and tone made it obvious that she thought I had played a part in the situation. I hadn't and was sorry for what happened. She was an attractive, vivacious woman, who had arrived in our town the year before as both a new teacher and divorcee, which had to have figured in.

Thanks to her experience, I learned that politics, gossip, and jealousy can seriously damage a person's reputation and career. It was a lesson that I never forgot. It showed me that people can be blamed for something they didn't do, and that life isn't always fair. It happened to my classmate, and certainly happened to her—and then she blamed me, at least in part. That wasn't fair either. It was my first taste of injustice.

These things, memories from long ago, visit me tonight—fragmented parts of what I've experienced—the good, the bad and everything in-between—with volumes more as I keep going. It's life, and it's hard at times. I wonder how people make it without faith and the hope for something better. For now, while I'm here, I trust God to always be with me, through it all.

Joshua 1:9 For the LORD your God is with you wherever you go.

WORDS NEVER SPOKEN

They are gone now,
taken at a rippled pace,
amid the drabness or the dickering
of ordinary days.
While here I remain,
to regard opportunities
I will never have again.
Moments of greeting
that called for the right word or more,
something agreeable,
a thank you or lavish hello.
Conversations of meaning,
candor mixed with pleasantries,
exchanges to bestow—
said with thoughtful ease.
Did they sense,
those of my heart gone on,
how this would someday feel?
Words never spoken
remain close to me,
wanting to be said,
needing to be heard.
I hope to say them someday.
But for now,
God knows the sound of them,
He knows every word.

Psalm 19:14 Let the words of my mouth and the meditation of my heart be acceptable to you, O Lord, my rock and my redeemer.

THE HEAVENLY SIDE

My father letting go
is a moment that I still behold—
his final breath a downward slide.
I watched him, quietly—
as a young girl, at his side.
Yet it was an older woman
giving her goodbye
to an even older man.
And who but God
could watch this sight
and truly understand.
His very breath expended
in a lifetime of events,
great, mundane, distressing,
as there, it met its end.
I think of that moment,
when he traveled from my grasp,
with a sweetened sadness
for the quickness of the path.
While I rejoice in the divine moment
of his letting go that night,
when he moved, peacefully, serenely,
to the heavenly side.

John 5:24 Very truly, I tell you, anyone who hears my word
and believes Him who sent me has eternal life, and does not
come under judgment, but has passed from death to life.

Marti Wells-Smith

MY HEART

I sleep, but my heart is awake,
in a night-filled room
where shadows move within
the stirring of a fan;
and street lights stare vaguely
through the parted, dusty blinds.
I move slowly at an ancient site,
tossed to my side
in a turn of piled sheets—
breathing the forgotten air
of distant reveries.
I awake to feel Him here,
my Heart, my Love,
standing close by, as the room grows light,
almost within touch
and just out of sight.

Song of Solomon 7:10 I am my beloved's, and His desire is
for me.

ALIVE

Here is my story
of an alluring guise;
fragile and frayed—
fraught with lies.
A coddling, deceptive path—
something to lament
if only I had.
For years I trudged upon it,
knowing it was wrong.
Yet I let it take me
where I never belonged…
And now here,
on this page, this night,
I tell you of the forgiven,
the forgotten things of God.
How I grow in faith—
Spirit to spirit.
How I move freely in Christ, quickened, alive;
How I now tread in the land of the living.

Psalm 116:7-9 Return, oh my soul, to your rest, for the LORD has dealt bountifully with you. For you have delivered my soul from death, my eyes from tears, my feet from stumbling. I walk before the LORD in the land of the living.

Marti Wells-Smith

THE DARKENED MIRROR

Behind the veil, gauzed and draped,
Your majesty was hidden.
Christ tore it, yes,
and with the tearing, entrance gained.
Yet we of the flesh cannot see your face
though the way is clearly made.
Your Word alive,
Your presence sensed.
Still, we must wait.
The mirrored view is dark, my Lord,
as we anticipate.
To know,
as we are known by You.
To see the light of Your countenance
take form as we approach.
Someday, Lord, someday
You will bless us with so much more.

1 Corinthians 13:12 For now we see in a mirror, dimly, but
then we will see face to face. Now I know only in part; then I
will know fully, even as I have been fully known.

MY MOTHER, WHO SAT IN A CHAIR

Mother, in her blue cotton robe, with a bifocaled gaze fixated somewhere beyond the maple trees out front, would lounge for hours each day on the screened-in porch of our old three-story home. This was a ritual of her later years, when family outcomes were clear, and both mistakes and gratitude could be mulled over without interruption.

She mentally surveyed us, appraising our lives in relation to her own. In between sips of coffee, she would also glance at her flowering plants and the hummingbirds that feasted on sugar water just outside the doorway.

Mother would often touch her cane as it leaned upon the old wicker rocker that my grandparents had first owned. Cars drove by, people walked up and down the sidewalk, dogs barked in the background. But it didn't distract her as she steadily rocked, sometimes notating in a journal, sometimes resting her eyes in the afternoon heat.

I would visit her there, listening to stories of the depression, her complaints of old age and her concerns for each of her three children. She raised us with strict discipline, filling in for Dad, who worked long hours as he moved upward in his company. He was kind and diligent. But Mother was the strongest one, who directed the details of our growing up in the very house where Father had been born and raised without want of any kind.

"I was dirt poor, happy to get an orange and some mittens for Christmas. We would have been a welfare family if the system had existed then."

It was disturbing to imagine my mother starving for fresh fruit and having only hand me downs to wear to her rural Kansas school. Her life had not lacked basics or a fair amount of luxuries since her marriage, but her recollections were staunch. Mother's life had lacked many things in her earlier years, and it carried over into her adult life.

"Mom, I wish I could make you laugh."

She had become more reclusive due to health issues and a growing sadness that made smiling a rarity. Dad would assist her on a daily basis, and then escape into a parallel universe that involved hobbies and projects, meetings and errands. Although there was genuine caring on both their parts, it was tempered with the long-accepted realization that they were very different from each other. Regardless of the undercurrent, my parents stayed together for many reasons, including their faith and family. They met on the porch as needed.

Mom responded to any known actions of her family with a sobering look if they were not as she thought best—and always fearing the worst, attempted to guide, fret, embrace and regret all within the same day. It must have been exhausting to hold us all in her mind and heart as she undoubtedly asked herself the question of *what if* as she considered *if only*.

"Martha, I had hoped you would never divorce. But here we go again."

She searched in scriptures daily to try and understand the deeper things of life. A woman who knew her prime in the 1950s, she later confessed to a deep frustration that she had used too much of her time shopping for dinner bargains at the local grocery store, drifting mentally as she mopped, dusted and folded laundry. Maxine, or Max, as her friends called her, moved within a generation of homemakers, the owners of feminine Sunday hats and belted A-line dresses, with bright lipstick and longings that were both unspoken and unfulfilled.

She fought her feelings of inferiority with a schedule of meetings and clubs, participating in church dinners, bridge parties and school activities. Mother was known for her excellent memory and beautiful face. Even with years of worry as she watched mistakes playing out in each of our lives, her face remained unlined until her dying day. Before her slow downfall began, she was also a woman with extraordinary pie baking skills, and would delight us with her creations for every occasion. She laughed in those days, teasing and visiting with neighbors and friends. Then, the first diagnosis.

"It's just a small lump, that's all."

But the cure for that led to other sinister findings. Perhaps it was the radiation that made it difficult for her to walk. Her prayers and Bible studies intensified through the years as she struggled to gain a sense of inner peace. In one of our last visits, Mother told me that she had finally come to accept her imperfections and the inescapable flaws of this fleshly life—all of it transpiring from the wicker chair on the porch where her mornings began and her days ended.

It had become a small, comfortable place in the universe. Surrounded by her beloved books, she traveled the world from that chair, and into the heavenly places, too. I find my own sense of peace in knowing that she also dreamed in that spot, and that some of them came true.

Philippians 4:12-13 I know what it is to have little, and I know what it is to have plenty. In any and all circumstances I have learned the secret of being well-fed and of going hungry, of having plenty and of being in need. I can do all things through Him who strengthens me.

Marti Wells-Smith

A MEMORIZED PRAYER

Sometimes we raced from our church,
bells ringing out in a smooth, steady pace,
past Father and Mother, who sauntered away.
Hurriedly changing, flinging our clothes
in a careless and childish array.
The day, it was waiting, amazing and new—
we moved in its realm with great laughter.
Sunday dinner, soon to be served,
the power of it keeping us there.
Mother's creations, practiced, performed
upon skillets that simmered her craft;
as we jabbered and jostled,
clamoring for chairs,
begging for pie and the park.
Our lives were unmarked, a memorized prayer
that we spoke in half whispers and rhyme.
There was no way of grasping
the course of our years,
mistakes that would surface in time—
or pain to surpass a loud reprimand—
understanding had not yet arrived.
Thinking the world to be ours, only ours,
before innocence said its good bye.
We knew little then,
but, in asking again,
we did go to the park and eat pie.

1 Corinthians 13:11 When I was a child, I spoke like a child,
I thought like a child, I reasoned like a child; when I became
an adult, I put an end to childish ways.

SPARROWS

House sparrows swoop and hide
in the old holly bush to the side of my porch;
clustered with berries
and sharp-edged leaves
that never turn dull or lifelessly fall.
A place for small flocks to tuck in their wings
when rain pours upon them
or snow settles in.
These sparrows that scatter and fearfully fly
from the young, rumpled boys who often pass by
and the chattering girls who follow behind,
never, not once, see the woman inside.
I perch in the background,
hidden away
with a lap of white paper
and rambling thoughts—
of what is, and could be
but simply is not…
And the sparrows, they console me,
as I sit, watching God
move upon their lives—
providing every need.

Matthew 10:31 So do not be afraid; you are of more value
than many sparrows.

OLD WOMAN OF CAREY STREET*

Her chair makes a groan, alarming the cat,
who leaps to a table turned dull with age—
surrounded by lace and rows of young faces
that only this woman could know.
She steadily rocks,
gazing with interest on framed, smiling lips—
as slowly, they each start to move;
afternoon sun basking within
the soft, aching blue of her eyes.
Caressing need, ageless want
sleepwalk and stagger to life.
They beckon her near, with God standing by.
"Join us," they earnestly say.
"Yes…" she responds. "Oh yes.
We will travel the years, making our way
to times of new joy and old peace."
Dusk arrives early—
must she let go?
Those of her heart gather close.
Laughing she stays,
past the stroke of return
in the year that had pleased her the most.

2 Corinthians 4:16 So we do not lose heart. Even though
our outer nature is wasting away, our inner nature is being
renewed day by day.

Revised - First published in Gifts of Words 1990

RED, THE BUM

I grew up on Pine Street, in a small Kansas community that was a county seat. Columbus had a downtown square that surrounded the old brick courthouse, with its turn of the century charm that included a jail on the third floor. A variety of shops and stores were on all sides, with my favorites being the 5&10, a drug store with an old-fashioned soda fountain and two cafes specializing in home cooking. It was almost perfect as I look back. There were containers filled with seasonal flowers placed near Victorian looking street lamps, none of which were ever vandalized or stolen. They are still intact to my knowledge.

In the 50's and early 60's, folks didn't bother to lock their doors at night. Nothing had happened yet to change the tradition of trust, although there were a few who served time for minor infractions. I could ride my bike to town safely, or maybe walk and skip with my allowance clutched in a coin purse. The dress shop was too expensive for me, but a quarter could really get something at the dime store—candy, trinkets, maybe a balloon and some gum. It was a good atmosphere for a child or family, or anyone who preferred a more rural lifestyle.

There were receded entranceways on the square with stairs leading up to apartments, where balconies jutted out from the living rooms and tall windows fluttered with old curtains. I would often see him sitting on a bottom stair, in sight, but barely. He was known as Red, or as others called him, Red the Bum. He had scraggly, sandy-red hair, kind eyes, and a harmless, toothless grin. He wore suspenders, long sleeve shirts and knee-high rubber boots year-round.

"Hi, kid. Can you spare a nickel?"

"Sorry, Red. I just spent it all on candy. Want some?"

He grinned and nodded, and I dug into my paper bag for a soft, cherry flavored nugget. He unwrapped it slowly and popped it into the side of his mouth.

"Thanks. You're a nice little girl. See you next week, maybe."

"You hopping a train again, Red?"

He shrugged his shoulders and I started walking away, wondering about him as I went. Why was he homeless? Where did he sleep at night? I saw him get a handout at the bakery once. Maybe he did dishes or picked up fallen change on the sidewalks by the bank. Maybe he was once a big shot and something happened that changed his life forever. I had quite an imagination. Dad said nobody really knew— he would simply show up in town and come and go as he wanted.

"Martha Lou, he's just an old man who used to ride box cars during the depression. I think he still does."

Months passed and Red continued to wander around. I would see him at the park, or the pool, or meandering down side streets near Main. We would wave as he shuffled by. He looked thinner to me, and had developed a limp. Somebody told me the motel owner sometimes gave him a room if he took out trash and did odd jobs.

Meanwhile, I moved on to junior high as people got married, babies were born, and others said their goodbyes before being ceremoniously buried at the town cemetery. I could feel things changing as I daydreamed about true love. On the surface, it was still a small-town utopia, but cracks had appeared and secrets were exposed. Scandals were discussed in private, and gossip thrived as political unrest and widespread disenchantment and rebellion emerged.

I probably asked my mother a hundred questions about life in general. Some things just didn't make sense.

"Mom, why did Mr. Frazier say that babies go to hell if they die before being baptized?"

"Mr. Frazier is wrong, dear. Babies don't go to hell."

I overheard him say it in our living room that week. He was an upstanding member of the Presbyterian Church we attended two blocks over. I also saw him being snide to Red two days later by the hardware store.

Of course, the day came when Red was nowhere to be found. I was glad then, that I had been nice to him and smiled back when he did. To this day, I still wonder where he came from and what happened to him. He was a sweet old man, who probably grew up poor and maybe neglected too, and he most likely didn't receive a ceremonious burial. He's forgotten by most, and was overlooked by many, but to me, Red is unforgettable. I like to think that he hopped one last train and just kept going.

Luke:20 Blessed are you who are poor, for yours is the kingdom of God.

MESSAGES

The eyes, most of all, tell a story,
liquid or hard,
a flick of a shine
or a dart from within.
It is good, bad, something bright or dim,
but we see it,
elation or grief—
as the mouth is curving
or drawn tight and thin.
The body, too,
as shoulders stoop,
or pull back and lock—
as fingers point
or gesture us near.
Signs of love, disdain,
anger, need,
or something undefined
that can heal or bleed.
And the mind,
it holds these moments,
sometimes clearly,
sometimes in forgetfulness.
Something is right or wrong
in these messages from the heart,
and only God knows the fullness of the story.

Psalm 44:21 Would not God discover this? For He knows the secrets of the heart.

BURDEN OF CARE

We gather both joy and pain
as we travel along the cobbled way.
I find the mixture to be glorious,
ravaging, too.
A concoction of many stories,
with a myriad of views.
I am drawn to the people
who stand to the side,
heads down, eyes that sigh.
Their struggles yet untold,
their spirits surely tried.
Look at me, dear woman, left alone—
for I have been there in your place.
I know the tears, the fear of nothing more
that greets your life as you hobble on.
Grief at your shoulder like a plague of doubt,
wild and pointless in its disarray—
bombarding you with what went wrong…
Step forward, dear man, with your failure looming,
with nothing to stop the mistake once made—
the moment of action too long delayed.
Yearning for what you had,
or almost had
or mindlessly threw away.
Let me hold your burden of care,
for I am assured
that it grows lighter by His grace.
Turn to me and let me feel your pain.
There is comfort in sharing and trying again.

Galatians 6:2 Bear one another's burdens, and in this way
you will fulfill the law of Christ.

THE SNUB

Life is such a mixture of things. As soon as I was old enough to comprehend the strangeness of it, and the beauty too, I began to store my memories in different compartments, with a hidden one for things worth forgetting. I learned early on that our emotions can lift us to great heights or dash us to fragments as we move through ordinary days into the extraordinary.

An example of both took place on a beautiful autumn morning around 38 years ago. The maples were rich with reds and burgundies, mingled with bright oranges and yellows. Those colors made me sigh and smile. I viewed the richness of them, scattered between the green leaved branches of other trees, and thanked God for such beauty.

To this day, I continue to enjoy the height of the season—coasting through fall scenery, or slowly walking around. The incident happened while I was home for a visit. I had decided to amble through the small Kansas town where I was born and raised. I saw a woman approaching me who had been a classmate of mine in high school.

"Hello, Sandy."

She abruptly turned her head the other way and kept walking. It was a snub, and on such a beautiful day. I kept walking too, with an abrupt, sickened feeling. When our eyes had met, I briefly saw the glare in hers. A few years had passed since graduation, but our looks hadn't changed. She knew it was me. Funny how your mind will reel and start extracting all the possible reasons why something just happened.

We had rarely moved in the same circles, and I had no idea of the coldness between us until then. I instantly wondered if she had rejected me based on my silly persona from school days, or perhaps on rumors and half-truths. I considered the fact that she may never have liked what little she knew of me. It struck a lifelong, insecure nerve, which I countered by reminding myself of good friends and nice memories, of gaining a degree, of finally marrying the right man, of holding down a decent job—and of always trying to be nice to people. Still, the nerve pounded.

I found myself reaching into the secret compartment that holds things I regret. Things that I hope others don't know, that I asked forgiveness of long ago. I wondered what she knew and consoled myself with the fact that no one is without regret, or mistakes.

It was never resolved and I never saw her again. But it made the colors fade that day. And try as I might, I can't keep the memory of it fully contained in my hidden, forgotten compartment.

Matthew 7:1 Do not judge, so that you may not be judged.

TRUTH

In times gone by,
the music would reach out,
becoming a world of its own.
The unknowing of what lies ahead
a soft shield to cushion my bed,
and the many dreams upon it.
As a reckless girl, I danced in my head,
And spun thoughts of greatness
and youthful desire.
I lived in the song as it played—
Earth, Wind and Fire—
on and on, eyes closed and flamed,
lacing hopes into a sound
that only I could hear.
While the purpose of my life
would remain out of sight,
and be hidden for many years...
If I could go back to my time of youth,
I would fill myself with Your lasting truth—
and change...almost everything.
But that too, is only a dream.
Instead, I trust You to move me forward,
and see what that will bring.

1 Peter 5:10 And after you have suffered for a little while, the God of all grace, who has called you to His eternal glory in Christ, will Himself restore, support, strengthen, and establish you.

UNDER LAYER THREE

Some of it is euphoric,
some shady, tucked in pain.
A collage of memories
that transfer and surprise,
sifting through this believer's mind.
She runs upon a path
much different than most,
as she struggles with the course
of her calling.
Few will understand
how it works—
this thing called her heart—
the upward climb, or the falling.
Much is stored under layer three,
that she hides upon a secret shelf.
I know that God forgives her—
now she must forgive herself.

Colossians 3:13 ...just as the Lord has forgiven you, so you also must forgive.

SUDDENLY, AT 15

Perhaps each of us have known someone who passed through this life rather quickly, yet left a lasting impression that brings them to mind again and again. Kristy Overman was just such a person. She was a small-town Kansas girl with timeless beauty and a sincere sweetness that left no one begrudging her the title of school princess or a position as class officer. It was expected for her, and given to her as a rightful place among her peers.

Kristy's family was in a position to lavish her with every advantage, and she was someone who would have undoubtedly done well in life, regardless of the path she chose. I was a classmate and admirer, along with all the others. The fact that she spoke to me, acknowledged me in the hallways and invited me to her home on occasion, was nectar for someone who was unquestionably an outsider.

"Want to come to my party this weekend?"

I emphatically nodded yes. I always wanted to go. Who didn't? And it was a nice one, of course. She made me feel welcome that night, along with a mix of other young people from different backgrounds, with a wide array of personalities. We all had one thing in common, though. We were naïve—ignorant, really—of what life was all about and how it could change in a heartbeat.

Kristy and I had a few moments alone in her bathroom as I watched her brush her brown, flipped up hair and apply pale pink lipstick. The mirror was huge, like her smile. She spoke to me as if I were her best friend, although I wasn't.

"Are you trying out for the play, Marti?"

I struck a pose. "Maybe for Stupefyin' Jones."

I was dramatic, corny at times, with a nice enough life of my own, just minus the tiara and closet full of designer clothes. She didn't care though. That was the inner beauty of the girl—Kristy met you in the middle, accepting and generous.

She left the room with a laugh and I followed, wanting the moment to last longer. She was soon swallowed up by the crowd, and I wandered the outskirts of the party for the rest of the night, trying to fit in.

The school year continued and for one reason or another, we didn't connect much after that. When it came to a close, I felt the same relief as everyone else—finding the break especially welcome that particular summer. My parents had agreed to let me attend a drama camp at MSU in Springfield, and it was a big deal to me.

Toward the middle of training sessions and rehearsals, however, my mom called.

"Honey, I have some bad news. Kristy Overman died."

My breath caught and I went blind for a moment. I envisioned a horrific car accident or airplane crash. "What? How?"

"She died in her sleep. They're having an autopsy performed before the funeral."

I couldn't grasp it. It took everything I had to stay with the play and see it through. My parents had spent hard earned money to send me there. I was a state away in Missouri with the responsibility of performing. They thought I should finish it, and I reluctantly did.

I found out on the second call that her heart had given out.

Suddenly, at 15, she was gone—it turned out that she had an unknown heart condition that had given no warning signs. Just like that, Kristy Overman died and went to heaven, where she would undoubtedly be even more of an angelic presence than she was here. "She's now in a beautiful place," many said, but it made life seem precarious to me at a time when I hadn't questioned the uncertainty of it. Friends told me the funeral was massive and that sobbing teenagers, including themselves, had passed by her white casket, surrounded by pale pink roses, shaking their heads in disbelief. Everyone felt the shock of it, the finality of such an unexpected loss.

I returned to what looked like my old hometown, the only place I'd ever really known, but something seemed altered. It was in the air—I could sense it, feel it all around me. Things really could change in a heart-beat. Important, unforgettable things. Kids were still dragging Main, still going to the drive-in to flirt as they ordered malts and kicked around plans for their futures, but it wasn't quite the same and never would be.

There have been other sad times, and good ones, too, that have been life altering as the years go on. Yet there is something about Kristy. Decades after she left, I still remember her with great fondness and wonder what she's doing today in Paradise.

Matthew 5:8 Blessed are the pure in heart, for they will see God.

THE LONG, LONG PATH

I stroll among the rows of faded epitaphs,
through gray stone monuments, ornately formed,
with a scattering of slate pillars, erected on each side—
their scrolled, mossy words darkened by time.
Cherubs and winged angels endlessly caress,
while guarding the history below—
weathered, chipped angels, who never speak—
will not reveal their memories.
Yet in the softness of this hour,
I think of each soul who once lived in flesh,
if only for a year or two,
if only for a day.
Perhaps Godly, purposed lives for some—
and those who had once, faithfully, visited each grave.
Then a turn to the right, where her husband inscribed,
"Walk slowly down the long, long path, until you hear
me call your name."
If only her angel could confide
what happened all those years ago.
But her fate remains buried
and I will never know.

Ecclesiastes 12:7 And the dust returns to the earth as it was,
and the breath returns to God who gave it.

HOLDING IT IN

This heaviness, that will not go away—
hanging on, with its troubling thoughts,
at 2 a.m., again at 10;
like an angered response,
sulking and grim.
If bringing it forward
will help or heal,
then out with it—
the coiled secret never told,
left to smolder your thoughts
or crowd your soul.
The unspoken need,
the unanswered question,
let it erupt
or quietly come forth.
Let it step outside,
into a place where others cannot hear
and thoughtlessly repeat.
With purposed intent, lift it to God;
let go and be released.

1 Peter 5:7 Cast all your anxiety on him, because he cares for you.

MOUNTAIN TOP

The drive was surrounded by aspens and evergreens as we wound up Pikes Peak, slowly moving between its terrain as both sides of the road stayed covered in sunlight. It poured upon the tops of wooded areas, skimming above the recesses of the land. I shifted and turned to take it in as we kept going.

A large hawk moved just in front of us, flying from a perch on one side of the road to the other. He moved as though we didn't exist, fearless and free. It felt like a holy place then, a place where God smiled as He created it. I let my mind drift for a moment as we traveled, picturing Him as He called forth countless designs and terrains—textures, sizes, shapes and purposes, all of it ours to enjoy, to pursue and explore in our earthly home.

Such greatness was beyond me. I felt nameless and invisible, longing to connect with the magnificence of that place in a way that could be captured and held, but I knew that a memory album would be the closest I'd get.

"Go even slower, honey. I want to take another pic."

A minute later, my lungs didn't want to expand as I struggled with the rhythm of breathing. The air was thin and shallow as my husband and I took a break at 12,000 feet. Lightheaded and shaken, I opened my door and sat on the edge of my seat, gasping. It was then that I noticed a dead bird laying near pinecones scattered to the right of the car. His black feathered body was still plump and perfectly formed. I wondered about his demise—was it an illness, or old age? Did we frighten a predator away with our arrival? I hoped that his mate mourned his passing and that it was a quick, gallant death.

It was then that I realized we shouldn't go any further. We both looked a little pale, and it was obvious that the altitude was affecting us.

I reluctantly said, "I think you need to turn around. I can't catch my breath."

Still moving slowly, we changed direction and went down the mountainside, continuing to enjoy the view, but with the sure knowledge that we would never attempt it again. Perhaps we had waited too long for this Colorado goal to be fulfilled. Older lungs and a more cautious approach to life gave us both reasons to alter our plans and descend.

Later, in the hotel room, I recalled our breathtaking day, a day where I had seen abundant life in all its glory, and death too. I alternated between reproaching myself for quitting and rationalizing why it was necessary.

After all, I thought, what's wrong with ascending part of a great mountain? What would be bad about choosing a smaller one the next time? Even the smallest would still be something that holds its own measure of beauty, and we could breathe easy on the journey.

Isaiah 54:10 For the mountains may depart and the hills be removed, but my steadfast love shall not depart from you…

RANGE OF EMOTION

The first cry, whimpered,
then the next, bold and rich.
Later, a broadened smile
and laughter, too.
Then more times of helplessness,
with pride in learning,
while sad for the losing.
Love that takes its place
amid sorrow on all sides;
anger, sometimes at life itself,
fear that grips your pulse.
This range of emotion
that overcomes us
at any given time—
it is a spectrum of great depth and height.
In it, I, too, have felt moments of defeat
and at times, nothing at all,
before seeking His intervention
and heeding the Spirit's call.

Galatians 5:22-23 By contrast, the fruit of the Spirit is love, joy, peace, patience, kindness, generosity, faithfulness, gentleness and self-control...

TALKING TO THE AIR

I've seen them often—old men and aged women, who mutter to themselves when they think no one is looking. They turn on the side streets of my town with bowed heads. They appear to watch their shoes move, or count the cracks in the sidewalk, while they quietly mumble about their day.

Many have curved backs and thinning hair, covered with frayed caps or faded floral scarves. Some seem to be saddened by unpleasant encounters, perhaps years of them. Others are harder to read, with little half-smiles that appear to be drawn on their faces. I know some of them by name, and have waved as I drive by, but they usually appear too preoccupied to respond, or they don't notice.

There are younger ones, too, who seem to be lost—meandering around the downtown area as if they've forgotten where they're going. I've thought about all of them often. *These souls are my brothers and sisters in Christ. Do they need help? Should I do something?*

During my years of crisis work, I tried to help many kinds of people, for every conceivable reason. I took it seriously, but for every person I was able to provide with needed services, there were others who chose to do the same things over and over again.

"John, I can help you get into rehab. It's a good program. It works."

"Tried it before, no thanks."

"Susan, I can arrange for a Safe House. You don't have to take his abuse."

"But I love him. He's promised to change."

On it went, years of it, but then there were clients who did rise above their circumstances, and those were the ones who kept me going. They just needed help with rent, or a job resume. Maybe they needed parenting skills or a resource for utility bills. Sometimes they just wanted someone they could trust, someone who would listen and not judge.

I drove them to court and the grocery store, to admissions to sign up for college courses and to other regional agencies to try and access more assistance. Although I worked in the mental health field, most of my clients were simply distressed individuals who were desperate for additional support. I had developed a list of help agencies and organizations in my area that provided basic needs, and more times than not, we were able to resolve what was wrong, or at least part of it.

A few of my former clients are related to the very people that I still see walking aimlessly around town. What are they murmuring? They look as if they're talking to the air, and actually, I can relate. I try to be subtle, waiting until I'm alone. My whispered comments are said on my front porch, or while I do dishes or take a bath.

"Why would she say that to me? Good Lord, I should have had a good comeback."

"I have to lose weight. Mind over matter."

"I need a break. This is too hard."

Always, it ends in silent prayer. *Please Lord, help me. Please, Father, help them, too.* Sometimes, the most ordinary things become overwhelming when enough piles together, and it turns into a crisis. Sometimes, there are extremely difficult situations. I've lived through many—divorce, death of a loved one, financial problems, health issues. I could truly relate to my clients at many levels.

If a client was feeling hopeless, I would silently pray for the opportunity to speak of faith, of the importance of it— the absolute necessity of it. But it wasn't something I could initiate. If it came out in conversation, then I would lightly proceed. My years in crisis case work had become a calling, and I would use my own life as an example of how God can intercede and help resolve even the most disastrous situations. This resonated with many, and it was deeply satisfying to me at a spiritual level.

When I was able to take early retirement, I did. But the time I spent with people who touched my heart—with stories of every kind of pain and hardship imaginable—has stayed with me. Although I still try to help when an opportunity presents itself, it remains difficult to witness the struggles of those around me, as well as on the national and global scenes. When I encounter troubled, lonely souls in the course of my day, I hope that they are doing more than talking to the air. I hope that they, too, are praying.

Psalm 74:21 Do not let the downtrodden be put to shame; let the poor and needy praise your name.

THE OTHER CHEEK

Words that slap,
haven't we all felt them?
The frowning strike,
the superbly placed sting,
a compelling price
for what truth will bring.
The other cheek turns,
but never in despair—
the pain is brief
as we're left standing there.
Then marching on,
to fertile ground
or weakened, starving sod,
we plant more seed
knowing full well
that the rest is up to God.

1 Corinthians 3:7 So neither the one who plants nor the one who waters is anything, but only God who gives the growth.

WISDOM ARRIVES

My life once turned in circles,
like rings upon water
when the stillness is disturbed.
It plunged and surged,
like an abstract page
drawn by a petulant child,
one with a tempered rage.
I stood in the company of likeable fools—
their example—my folly...
Yes, wisdom was late in arriving,
her invitation delayed.
Had I asked for her sooner,
my life would be different today.

Proverbs 8:1, 8:12 Does not wisdom call, and does not understanding raise her voice?...I, wisdom, live with prudence, and I attain knowledge and discretion.

THE SHINING FOREVER

DREAMING

In my dreams last night
you were close by, at my side.
It had a warmth to it,
a kindness that sat between us
as we took a ride
down our favorite country road.
Just like old times—
before you grew up
and before we knew
that life, here with us,
would not last long enough.
Late last night, we drove toward the moon.
It was wonderful to see you!
I hope God lets you return,
and very soon.

Isaiah 66:13 As a mother comforts her child, so I will comfort
you…

HAPPY

To feel it again,
no gravity, lifted, suspended—
upheld in weightless air.
Lesser feelings, cares,
covered with silk and put away.
Happiness—
it was never a feeling that stayed.
But it came often enough,
coaxed to remain,
sometimes for days on end.
It took nothing grand
to draw it in.
Arriving as refreshment,
to linger and sooth,
or as laughter,
with a bit of good news.
Lord, I long to be happy again,
if not here,
then in the hereafter.
But it is my joy that I pray will return.

Psalm 16:11 You show me the path of life. In Your presence there is fullness of joy; in Your right hand are pleasures forevermore.

Marti Wells-Smith

PEACE BE WITH ME

The quiet of tonight surrounds me,
its stillness, a place to rest.
Gone is this day of hurried steps,
the rush of ordered tasks.
I meditate as the candle flames
and exhale into its light.
Thoughts are hushed and calm,
my silent prayers among them.
There is a letting go, of what I've known
is not mine to control.
Your peace has come upon me.
I reach out, as You take hold.

John 14:27 Peace I leave with you; My peace I give to you.

IN TURNING BACK

The past is a place of our making.
To revisit what is pained
is to dwell upon sorrow—
echoes of turmoil,
hauntings of good bye—
when we were far from ready to let go.
Rather, let us embrace
the affection of another soul,
the importance of love,
of giving, one to another.
In turning back,
may only comfort be derived
from a tranquil reflection
of the many virtues in our lives.

Proverbs 10:7 The memory of the righteous is a blessing...

Marti Wells-Smith

THE LIMITS OF UNDERSTANDING

It is beyond my grasp,
this pulsing of life,
as it rushes through me
and around me—
always moving, onward bound.
Surely it is a gift,
but the Giver, a grand mystery.
The Great I Am,
told of in the Word,
felt by spirit,
received through grace.
God, the One who has always been.
And yet, how can that possibly be?
The limits of understanding are endless,
therefore, faith must intervene.

Proverbs 3:5 Trust in the Lord with all your heart, and do not rely on your own insight.

THE HEALING

I was healed once before,
years ago.
My arms raised in faith,
as You chose to remove the pain,
instantly.
A constant aching,
gone, in a moment's time…
This pain, not of flesh and bone,
is deeper, stronger,
than any I have ever known,
or ever will.
The constant aching has returned
and to my very core.
I raise my arms for healing,
asking, Lord, once more.

Psalm 30:2 O LORD my God, I cried to You for help, and
You have healed me.

SADNESS, LEAVING

Grief, in time,
is but a gentle missing;
a breath of want
for those gone on,
for those held dear—
a fond desire to bring them closer;
a wish to draw them near.
Sadness transforms,
making way for tomorrow,
as we each choose what will follow
in the aftermath of sorrow.

Matthew 5:4 Blessed are those who mourn, for they will be comforted.

Lamentations of the Heart

Always and Forever, Grant,
you are in my heart, my thoughts,
my memories.
For the rest of my life,
with unending love,
I will be remembering…*

John 3:16 For God so loved the world that He gave His only Son, so that everyone who believes in Him may not perish but may have eternal life.

Hebrews 2:4 While God added His testimony by signs and wonders and various miracles, and by gifts of the Holy Spirit, distributed according to His will.

*Excerpt from Facebook post 6-21-2020

Marti Wells-Smith

Kesler Photography Mound Valley KS

This 2011 high school graduation photo reminds me of how much Grant loved the ranch life. He enjoyed every aspect of it and was a natural. In his story, "The Greater of the Two," I share that he dreamed of an Oklahoma spread of his own someday. Yet, I know that his heavenly home is far grander than anything he could have hoped for here.

The following hymn lyrics, written by Horatio Spafford in 1873, were supernaturally used by the Lord to allow my son to give me a very special message. Only the first verse is reprinted here, because it was the repeating refrain that I was meant to take to heart that day. I write of the moment in Grant's story.

It Is Well With My Soul

When peace like a river attendeth my way
When sorrows like sea billows roll
Whatever my lot, Thou hast taught me to know
It is well, it is well with my soul.

It is well (it is well)
With my soul (with my soul)
It is well, it is well, with my soul.

Merl Humphrey Photography, Fort Scott, KS

This is the heart shaped profile rock that is my tangible gift and sign–written of in Grant's story, *The Greater of the Two*. You can see the incredible similarity between our photo and the rock itself, with my son's story explaining the timing and significance of its appearance. I treasure it and thank God for the eternal love that it represents.

Portions from *Daniel* 6: 26 and 27…For He is the living God, enduring forever…He delivers and rescues, He works signs and wonders in heaven and on earth…

Marti Wells-Smith

About the Author

Marti Wells-Smith is a Christian, wife, friend, and grieving mother, who finds great hope in continuing her life journey amid unexpected joy and sadness. She shares her deepest thoughts and experiences through free verse poetry and non-fictional prose to comfort others who struggle with the loss of a child or loved one, or with life itself.

She's a native Kansan who advocates for people in need as well as animals, large and small. Her background includes being a past board member for a local mother to mother ministry, safehouse and no kill animal shelter, as she continues to raise funds for the shelter at a local antique/thrift store. Her daily routine includes caring for her adopted lab mix and three devoted cats.

Marti was involved in all fine arts that were offered during her school years and participated in local and regional theater productions well into her adulthood.

She received a BA in English and Sociology from Pittsburg State University, Pittsburg, Kansas, and began her career with jobs that included being a copy and feature writer in both radio and regional and state-wide news publications. She won state and national awards for human interest stories during her years as editor and writer for a large electrical cooperative in Oklahoma, and has had poetry published in Home Life, the anthology Gifts of Words and Western Horseman.

Marti made a mid-life career change to crisis services before pursuing writing fulltime again. She now seeks solace in faith and fellowship, her husband Scott and their extended family. and is often seen sitting quietly on her sunporch, wondering about what could have been, and is yet to be.

Marti can be found at her website: martiwellssmith.com
Email: marti@martiwellssmith.com

Other MSI Memoirs

CPSIA information can be obtained
at www.ICGtesting.com
Printed in the USA
BVHW040018260221
601130BV00004B/872

9 781950 328758